Head In The Clouds

Erin Walker

Dedication

For all those fighting to be dreamers
in an ever-practical world.

Contents

1

Just One Thing

Just one thing before we begin:

I am a dreamer,

And I will always dream.

2

We have all the right answers to all the wrong questions.

3

Who ever thought that shackles could be beautiful?

I am bound, but I am not afraid. I am in prison, but I am not deprived.

Art is a rope that holds my limbs, a beautiful rope that holds me in place.

What a simple thing intricacy is, that music should hold me captive. What a beautiful thing my chains are, that they should guard me from silence.

4

Written Sonata

Don't want to close my eyes. Don't want to fall asleep. Dreaming, eyes open. Entranced as if glued to this moment—my heart belongs to you. Take me, music. Take me, musician, to the passages of your heart. Whispering, we fade together... and the thought is gone.

5

Birds

Oh, what I would give to be one of those which fly amongst falling heaven.

6

Why would I take a step inward

To imagine a forest made of pure gold,

When to my left a ruddy yellow, no, look,

Sunlight dripped with sweet blood,

To my right fire opal, and behind it,

The yellow glisten of reflecting water,

And every falling whisp and gem,

Kissing my eyes, kissing my memory

7

Paint vividly. Don't hide the color. Don't blend the contrast.

8

You're the Sun

You're the sun

Too glittery for anyone to fully see

But I understand you—

You're worth so much

And not credited for half of what you do

Or what you are

9

Always Blue

The sky is always blue. When you think it isn't, that's just because the clouds are in the way.

10

Rain

As the sky falls from the sky, we listen with sucked in breath…
to miss a moment of this glory on earth, we would be fools.

11

Shall we assume that this is all there is to gain?

No...

Whispering tides,

A mist to heal the roots of severed green.

Should we wait for the outcome to come to us?

Perhaps...

But not now...

Just the hemming water,

Just the healing rain.

Peace, tranquil in the shadowed valley.

What is there to gain?

Purple like a bruised fruit,

But bare and untouched.

Deep color,

Precious stones.

Water...

Frigid, but why would we touch it...

Why would we touch it?

When we can watch it...

Unfolding, tumbling, sliding down the mountain.

12

A beacon of blue cleans the black from these nasty walls. Purity strikes evil like a hammer to an anvil. Sparks fly, the sword is finished. But is it conformed to the shape of the anvil, or of the hammer?

13

I expected that everything would stay the same, but forgot that there were seasons.

14

There has to be a better reason to keep breathing.

There has to be a better reason to get up in the morning.

There's got to be more to life than broken hearts and broken dreams.

15

You Changed Me

I used to only want to be strong

But then your arms held me

I used to think alone was fun

Until I felt the empty sheets

I used to think crying was weakness

Until the strongest I knew shed tears

I used to think I was smart

Until you showed me to be naive

I used to want what I couldn't have

And now I want it more than ever

You tell me I can have it

16

Feel this mortal breath on hands with immortal power.

17

Writing a book is like slowly wrapping a present for the whole world.

18

Imagination

Cracking.

Imagination--gone.

Hope--fading.

Love--lost.

Imagination gone.

Come back.

Come back.

19

Triangles...

Sleep...

Dots...

Disconnected thoughts...

Connected by a pen.

20

Writing poetry

When I shouldn't be

The curse of a writer

Is to want to dream

When we should be serious

21

There are only two things I hoard: friendships and paper.

22

This is How

This is how I don't forget. This is how I pour out my soul. This is how I scratch my blood onto a page. This is how I write.

23

The writer is always less brave than his character. Otherwise, he wouldn't have time to write--he would be *doing*.

24

If words were my being, I would be nothing but pages.

25

Paper for Rent

Too many secrets, too many lies

Too many wars fought with closed eyes

Too many times ignoring the pain

Too many times deciding to just remain

Too much syndrome in one pill

Too much time simply to kill

My blood smeared on the walls of this trap

Waiting until the fateful day I snap

In that blood, written a last will and testament:

Love, heartbreak, incomplete--paper for rent.

26

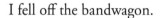

I fell off the bandwagon.

Like an addiction I can't shake, recovery only makes relapsing more difficult.

What's real stops mattering.

You look at me and see a girl who's always staring off into space...

As I try to overcome hallucinations that I create.

In my own mind, a web of horrors I can't break free of.

Help.

27

Dreamers

We look into the sun, knowing what can happen to our eyes. We fall in love, knowing what could happen to our hearts. We hope for the future, knowing we may not live another day. Why? Because we are dreamers.

28

Youth

They tell me I'm wasting my youth on you.

What's it matter if I waste my youth?

On them, on you,

On dreams that will never come true.

29

What is it worth to imagine fates never fated, to dream olden dreams, the beginnings of which have long passed?

30

The less you know, the more you can accomplish.

31

Wish on bulky cycle with like minds.

32

Practicality

You abandon love

for the sake of

Practicality.

You throw away peace

In the name of

Practicality.

You make your dreams

A last priority

And call it

Practicality.

You drive yourself insane,

And hurt those you love,

With no hopes to achieve.

You cry in your heart,

And somehow it's called

Practicality.

33

Practical

Your heart yearns to wander, but your wallet is here. Your plans are up North but your eyes are set below the equator. A fairytale lives in your mind, blinking, flashing, driving you mad, but you refuse to leave what you call reality.

You are never too young to do something great. You will never be too old to do what you dream. Why do you let yourself be tortured by what you don't have? Why do you make excuses to not do what you really want to? Why do you release your hold on your dreams for what's supposedly practical?

34

What am I doing? This isn't what I wanted. This is what they told me I *could* do. And maybe they were right. I could never live up to what I truly wanted to do with my life. The child who dreamed with golden eyes has died; this soldier with hardened chest remains. I stopped dreaming...I stopped growing. And now I'm headed for a *practical* life. The life they told me I *could* do...the life of talentless, colorless, monotonous me.

35

They will punish you the most for your best revenge - being happy, without having hurt anyone. Because the holders of leashes are the most bound there are, and those who dedicate themselves to making others suffer are the most miserable there are.

36

What is fantasy without reality?

Oh, but, darling, what is reality without fantasy?

37

For the first time in my life, I can smell the flowers, but they still don't smell sweet.

38

Do not become what you know you can be. Become what you know you can't be.

You won't know if you can do something until you've done it.

39

I know you could be anything that you want to be, because I believe that you can do anything you dream.

40

Dreams

I feel my life fading away.

Fingers trying to grasp something great,

Dreams.

Dreams of everything inconsequential.

Because none of it will *ever* happen.

I want to throw something—

Splinter wood,

Break bone,

Get everything bloody.

Unfinish the finished surfaces,

Destroy stained furniture.

Tear through the paintings I spent months on,

Set fire to the bed I sleep in alone.

Break the record player,

Destroy every memory of what keeps me here.

Stop watering the plants, let them grow,

Or die, among the rubble.

Shatter porcelain in my palm,

Bend the blade and make it break,

Drip paint across my fresh mess.

Tear strips of these hot blankets,

Throw to the ground this stiff chair,

Stomp holes in this abominably flat floor.

Tear these clothes.

I want out of these rigid lines,

This constricting hug,

These impossible walls.

Everything I wanted to do,

Want to do.

I wanted her to see what she inspired.

But she's gone now,

And she'll never see it,

If I even *do* it.

When I was a child,

My dreams were your dreams.

To be in the movies,

To wear pretty clothes on TV,

To write stories of drastic fates.

But now I'm not a child,

And your dreams have changed.

But mine haven't!

You don't care.

That's not practical,

Besides, you don't want to be famous.

That's not practical,

Besides, you don't want to have money.

That's not practical,

Besides, you don't want to have a career.

Suddenly my dreams are just dreams.

And what's practical is all I have to look forward to.

And all of a sudden you know what I want and I don't.

Apparently.

Write music,

Dance on tap shoes,

Hiphop, swing.

Be in a musical,

Start a business,

Build a website,

Publish a book,

Create something new,

Help a bunch of people

Just because I can.

Find true love,

Marry someone amazing.

Build a house,

Sit by a creek and write.

Be an artist,

Paint, sculpt, draw.

Choreograph.

Make a YouTube channel.

Write a blog.

Experiment with food.

Run for office.

Win.

Be the president.

Go to space.

Go to China.

Walk home in the dark.

Sing in the rain.

The dust settles and everything is as it was.

Finished, polished, smooth, straight.

Constricting.

It's not that I can't breathe.

It's that I can't break anything in this darned perfect world.

Go to college four years.

Meet someone who will never love you.

Marry him.

Get a job, then quit it.

Have three kids.

Send them to private school.

Marry them off.

The man you marry retires.

Travel the world.

Die of cancer.

Die of your life.

Throw away the manuscripts.

You can rip them up.

The only thing you can tear,

Your own heart.

Say goodbye to the dreams.

Say goodbye to that sweet childhood.

I want to go home.

Please give me my dreams,

So I can fail at them.

Please.

Please.

But this is all going nowhere.

Passions that no one else has, I have.

Ideas no one else can see, I visualize when I go to sleep.

I see red.

I see you.

You're blocking me.

You're refinishing everything I break.

And then you won't let me get lost.

What if I want to be lost?!

What if I want to cry?

What if I know that failure leads to greater success?

Unable to fail,

So unable to succeed.

Here's how my life ends...

I don't know.

And I was hoping for that,

Only for a different reason.

Somebody tell me why I can't break this room,

Tell me why I won't break myself,

Tell me what makes me compliant.

Tell me I can sleep at night,

Tell me I can dream in the morning,

And tell me those dreams are reality by sunset.

And then tell me I've failed,

So I can sleep in peace.

Because that means, someday,

I won't.

CPSIA information can be obtained
at www.ICGtesting.com
Printed in the USA
BVHW052250090223
658263BV00007B/303